William James

Human Immortality

Two supposed objections to the doctrine. Second Edition

William James

Human Immortality
Two supposed objections to the doctrine. Second Edition

ISBN/EAN: 9783337369705

Printed in Europe, USA, Canada, Australia, Japan

Cover: Foto ©Andreas Hilbeck / pixelio.de

More available books at **www.hansebooks.com**

HUMAN IMMORTALITY

TWO SUPPOSED OBJECTIONS
TO THE DOCTRINE

BY

WILLIAM JAMES

PROFESSOR OF PHILOSOPHY AT HARVARD UNIVERSITY, AND
INGERSOLL LECTURER FOR 1897–1898

SECOND EDITION

The Riverside Press

BOSTON AND NEW YORK
HOUGHTON, MIFFLIN AND COMPANY
The Riverside Press, Cambridge
1899

THE INGERSOLL LECTURESHIP

Extract from the will of Miss Caroline Haskell Ingersoll, who died in Keene, County of Cheshire, New Hampshire, Jan. 26, 1893.

First. In carrying out the wishes of my late beloved father, George Goldthwait Ingersoll, as declared by him in his last will and testament, I give and bequeath to Harvard University in Cambridge, Mass., where my late father was graduated, and which he always held in love and honor, the sum of Five thousand dollars ($5,000) as a fund for the establishment of a Lectureship on a plan somewhat similar to that of the Dudleian lecture, that is — one lecture to be delivered each year, on any convenient day between the last day of May and the first day of December, on this subject, "the Immortality of Man," said lecture not to form a part of the usual college course, nor to be delivered by any Professor or Tutor as part of his usual routine of instruction, though any such Professor or Tutor may be appointed to such service. The choice of said lecturer is not to be limited to any one religious denomination, nor to any one profession, but may be that of either clergyman or layman, the appointment to take place at least six months before the delivery of said lecture. The above sum to be safely invested and three fourths of the annual interest thereof to be paid to the lecturer for his services and the remaining fourth to be expended in the publishment and gratuitous distribution of the lecture, a copy of which is always to be furnished by the lecturer for such purpose. The same lecture to be named and known as "the Ingersoll lecture on the Immortality of Man."

PREFACE TO SECOND EDITION

SO many critics have made one and the same objection to the door-way to immortality which my lecture claims to be left open by the "transmission-theory" of cerebral action, that I feel tempted, as the book is again going to press, to add a word of explanation.

If our finite personality here below, the objectors say, be due to the transmission through the brain of portions of a preëxisting larger consciousness, all that can remain after the brain expires is the larger consciousness itself as such, with which we should thenceforth be perforce reconfounded, the only means of our existence in finite personal form having ceased.

But this, the critics continue, is the

pantheistic idea of immortality, survival, namely, in the soul of the world ; not the Christian idea of immortality, which means survival in strictly personal form.

In showing the possibility of a mental life after the brain's death, they conclude, the lecture has thus at the same time shown the impossibility of its identity with the personal life, which is the brain's function.

Now I am myself anything but a pantheist of the monistic pattern ; yet for simplicity's sake I did in the lecture speak of the "mother-sea" in terms that must have sounded pantheistic, and suggested that I thought of it myself as a unit. On page 30, I even added that future lecturers might prove the loss of some of our personal limitations after death not to be matter for absolute regret. The interpretation of my critics was therefore not unnatural ; and I ought to have been more careful to guard against its being made.

In note 5 on page 58 I partially guarded

against it by saying that the "mother-sea" from which the finite mind is supposed to be strained by the brain, need not be conceived of in pantheistic terms exclusively. There might be, I said, many minds behind the scenes as well as one. The plain truth is that *one may conceive the mental world behind the veil in as individualistic a form as one pleases, without any detriment to the general scheme by which the brain is represented as a transmissive organ.*

If the extreme individualistic view were taken, one's finite mundane consciousness would be an extract from one's larger, truer personality, the latter having even now some sort of reality behind the scenes. And in transmitting it — to keep to our extremely mechanical metaphor, which confessedly throws no light on the actual *modus operandi* — one's brain would also leave effects upon the part remaining behind the veil; for when a thing is torn, both fragments feel the operation.

And just as (to use a very coarse figure) the stubs remain in a check-book whenever a check is used, to register the transaction, so these impressions on the transcendent self might constitute so many vouchers of the finite experiences of which the brain had been the mediator; and ultimately they might form that collection within the larger self of memories of our earthly passage, which is all that, since Locke's day, the continuance of our personal identity beyond the grave has by psychology been recognized to mean.

It is true that all this would seem to have affinities rather with preëxistence and with possible re-incarnations than with the Christian notion of immortality. But my concern in the lecture was not to discuss immortality in general. It was confined to showing it to be *not incompatible* with the brain-function theory of our present mundane consciousness. I hold that it is so compatible, and compatible moreover in fully individualized form. The reader would be in accord with everything that the text of my lecture intended to say, were he to assert that every memory and affection of his present life is to be preserved, and that he shall never *in sæcula sæculorum* cease to be able to say to himself : " I am the same personal being who in old times upon the earth had those experiences."

HUMAN IMMORTALITY

T is a matter unfortunately too often seen in history to call for much remark, that when a living want of mankind has got itself officially protected and organized in an institution, one of the things which the institution most surely tends to do is to stand in the way of the natural gratification of the want itself. We see this in laws and courts of justice; we see it in ecclesiasticisms; we see it in academies of the fine arts, in the medical and other professions, and we even see it in the universities themselves.

Too often do the place-holders of such institutions frustrate the spiritual purpose to which they were appointed to minister, by the technical light which soon becomes the only light in which they seem able to see the purpose, and the narrow way which is the only way in which they can work in its service.

I confess that I thought of this for a moment when the Corporation of our University invited me last spring to give this Ingersoll lecture. Immortality is one of
V the great spiritual needs of man. The churches have constituted themselves the official guardians of the need, with the result that some of them actually pretend to accord or to withhold it from the individual by their conventional sacraments, — withhold it at least in the only shape in which it can be an object of desire. And now comes the Ingersoll lectureship. Its high-minded founder evidently thought that our University might serve the cause he had at heart more liberally than the churches do, because a university is a body so much less trammeled by traditions and by impossibilities in regard to choice of persons. And yet one of the first things

which the university does is to appoint a
man like him who stands before you, certainly not because he is known as an en-
thusiastic messenger of the future life,
burning to publish the good tidings to his
fellow-men, but apparently because he is
a university official.

Thinking in this way, I felt at first as if
I ought to decline the appointment. The
whole subject of immortal life has its prime
roots in personal feeling. I have to confess that my own personal feeling about
immortality has never been of the keenest
order, and that, among the problems that
give my mind solicitude, this one does not
take the very foremost place. Yet there
are individuals with a real passion for the
matter, men and women for whom a life
hereafter is a pungent craving, and the
thought of it an obsession; and in whom
keenness of interest has bred an insight
into the relations of the subject that no one
less penetrated with the mystery of it can
attain. Some of these people are known

to me. They are not official personages;
they do not speak as the scribes, but as
having direct authority. And surely, if
anywhere a prophet clad in goatskins, and
not a uniformed official, should be called to
give inspiration, assurance, and instruction,
it would seem to be here, on such a theme.
Office, at any rate, ought not to displace
spiritual calling.

And yet, in spite of these reflections,
which I could not avoid making, I am
here to-night, all uninspired and official as
I am. I am sure that prophets clad in
goatskins, or, to speak less figuratively, laymen inspired with emotional messages on
the subject, will often enough be invited
by our Corporation to give the Ingersoll
lecture hereafter. Meanwhile, all negative
and deadening as the remarks of a mere
professional psychologist like myself may
be in comparison with the vital lessons they
will give, I am sure, upon mature reflec-
tion, that those who have the responsibility
of administering the Ingersoll foundation

are in duty bound to let the most various kinds of official personages take their turn as well. The subject is really an enormous subject. At the back of Mr. Alger's 'Critical History of the Doctrine of a Future Life,' there is a bibliography of more than five thousand titles of books in which it is treated. Our Corporation cannot think only of the single lecture : it must think of the whole series of lectures *in futuro*. Single lectures, however emotionally inspired and inspiring they may be, will not be enough. The lectures must remedy each other, so that out of the series there shall emerge a collective literature worthy of the importance of the theme. This unquestionably was what the founder had in mind. He wished the subject to be turned over in all possible aspects, so that at last results might ponderate harmoniously in the true direction. Seen in this long perspective, the Ingersoll foundation calls for nothing so much as for minute division of labor. Orators must take their turn, and prophets ; but narrow specialists as well. Theologians of every creed, metaphysicians, anthropologists, and psychologists must alternate with biologists and physicists and psychical researchers,— even with mathematicians. If any one of them presents a grain of truth, seen from his point of view, that will remain and accrete with truths brought by the others, his will have been a good appointment.

In the hour that lies before us, then, I shall seek to justify my appointment by offering what seem to me two such grains of truth, two points well fitted, if I am not mistaken, to combine with anything that other lecturers may bring.

These points are both of them in the nature of replies to objections, to difficulties which our modern culture finds in the old notion of a life hereafter, — difficulties that I am sure rob the notion of much of its old power to draw belief, in the scientifically cultivated circles to which this audience belong.

The first of these difficulties is relative to the absolute dependence of our spiritual life, as we know it here, upon the brain. One hears not only physiologists, but numbers of laymen who read the popular science books and magazines, saying all about us, How can we believe in life hereafter when Science has once for all attained to proving, beyond possibility of escape, that our inner life is a function of that famous material, the so-called 'gray matter' of our cerebral convolutions? How can the function possibly persist after its organ has undergone decay?

Thus physiological psychology is what is supposed to bar the way to the old faith. And it is now as a physiological psychologist that I ask you to look at the question with me a little more closely.

It is indeed true that physiological science has come to the conclusion cited; and we must confess that in so doing she has only carried out a little farther the common belief of mankind. Every one knows that arrests of brain development occasion imbecility, that blows on the head abolish memory or consciousness, and that brain-stimulants and poisons change the quality of our ideas. The anatomists, physiologists, and pathologists have only shown this generally admitted fact of a dependence to be detailed and minute. What the laboratories and hospitals have lately been teaching us is not only that thought in general is one of the brain's functions, but that the various special forms of thinking are functions of special portions of the brain. When we are thinking of things seen, it is our occipital convolutions that are active ; when of things heard, it is a certain portion of our temporal lobes ; when of things to be spoken, it is one of our frontal convolutions. Professor Flechsig of Leipzig (who perhaps more than any one may claim to have made the subject his own) considers that in other special convolutions those processes of association go on, which permit the more abstract processes of thought, to take place. I could easily show you these regions if I had here a picture of the brain.[1] Moreover, the diminished or exaggerated associations of what this author calls the *Körperfühlsphäre* with the other regions, accounts, according to him, for the complexion of our emotional life, and eventually decides whether one shall be a callous brute or criminal, an unbalanced sentimentalist, or a character accessible to feeling, and yet well poised. Such special opinions may have to be corrected; yet so firmly established do the main positions worked out by the anatomists, physiologists, and pathologists of the brain appear, that the youth of our medical schools are everywhere taught unhesitatingly to believe them. The assurance that observation will go on to establish them ever more and more minutely is the inspirer of all contemporary research. And almost any of our young psychologists will tell you that only a few belated scholastics, or possibly some crack-brained theosophist or psychical researcher, can be found holding back, and still talking as if mental phenomena might exist as independent variables in the world.

For the purposes of my argument, now, I wish to adopt this general doctrine as if it were established absolutely, with no possibility of restriction. During this hour I wish you also to accept it as a postulate, whether you think it incontrovertibly established or not ; so I beg you to agree with me to-day in subscribing to the great psycho-physiological formula : *Thought is a function of the brain.*

The question is, then, Does this doctrine logically compel us to disbelieve in immortality ? Ought it to force every truly consistent thinker to sacrifice his hopes of an hereafter to what he takes to be his duty of accepting all the consequences of a scientific truth ?

Most persons imbued with what one may call the puritanism of science would feel themselves bound to answer this question with a yes. If any medically or psychologically bred young scientists feel otherwise, it is probably in consequence of that incoherency of mind of which the majority of mankind happily enjoy the privilege. At one hour scientists, at another they are Christians or common men, with the will to live burning hot in their breasts ; and, holding thus the two ends of the chain, they are careless of the intermediate connection. But the more radical and uncompromising disciple of science makes the sacrifice, and, sorrowfully or not, according to his temperament, submits to giving up his hopes of heaven.[2]

This, then, is the objection to immortality; and the next thing in order for me is to try to make plain to you why I believe that it has in strict logic no deterrent power. I must show you that the fatal consequence is not coercive, as is commonly imagined ; and that, even though our soul's life (as here below it is revealed to us) may be in literal strictness the function of a brain that perishes, yet it is not at all ✓ impossible, but on the contrary quite possible, that the life may still continue when the brain itself is dead.

The supposed impossibility of its continuing comes from too superficial a look at the admitted fact of functional dependence. The moment we inquire more closely into the notion of functional dependence, and ask ourselves, for example, how many kinds of functional dependence there may be, we immediately perceive that there is one kind at least that does not exclude a life hereafter at all. The fatal conclusion of the physiologist flows from his assuming offhand another kind of functional dependence, and treating it as the only imaginable kind.[3]

When the physiologist who thinks that his science cuts off all hope of immortality pronounces the phrase, " Thought is a function of the brain," he thinks of the matter just as he thinks when he says,

"Steam is a function of the tea-kettle," "Light is a function of the electric circuit," "Power is a function of the moving waterfall." In these latter cases the several material objects have the function of inwardly creating or engendering their effects, and their function must be called *productive* function. Just so, he thinks, it must be with the brain. Engendering consciousness in its interior, much as it engenders cholesterin and creatin and carbonic acid, its relation to our soul's life must also be called productive function. Of course, if such production be the function, then when the organ perishes, since the production can no longer continue, the soul must surely die. Such a conclusion as this is indeed inevitable from that particular conception of the facts.[4]

But in the world of physical nature productive function of this sort is not the only kind of function with which we are familiar. We have also releasing or permissive function; and we have transmissive function.

The trigger of a crossbow has a releasing function : it removes the obstacle that holds the string, and lets the bow fly back to its natural shape. So when the hammer falls upon a detonating compound. By knocking out the inner molecular obstructions, it lets the constituent gases resume their normal bulk, and so permits the explosion to take place.

In the case of a colored glass, a prism, or a refracting lens, we have transmissive function. The energy of light, no matter how produced, is by the glass sifted and limited in color, and by the lens or prism determined to a certain path and shape. Similarly, the keys of an organ have only a transmissive function. They open successively the various pipes and let the wind in the air-chest escape in various ways. The voices of the various pipes are constituted by the columns of air trembling as they emerge. But the air is not engendered in the organ. The organ proper, as distinguished from its air-chest, is only an apparatus for letting portions of it loose upon the world in these peculiarly limited shapes.

My thesis now is this : that, when we think of the law that thought is a function of the brain, we are not required to think of productive function only ; *we are entitled also to consider permissive or transmissive function.* And this the ordinary psycho-physiologist leaves out of his account.

Suppose, for example, that the whole universe of material things — the furniture of earth and choir of heaven — should turn out to be a mere surface-veil of phenomena, hiding and keeping back the world of genuine realities. Such a supposition is foreign neither to common sense nor to philosophy. Common sense believes in realities behind the veil even too superstitiously ; and idealistic philosophy declares the whole world of natural experience, as we get it, to be but a time-mask, shattering or refracting the one infinite Thought which is the sole reality into those millions of finite streams of consciousness known to us as our private selves.

> "Life, like a dome of many-colored glass,
> Stains the white radiance of eternity."

Suppose, now, that this were really so, and suppose, moreover, that the dome, opaque enough at all times to the full super-solar blaze, could at certain times and places grow less so, and let certain beams pierce through into this sublunary world. These beams would be so many finite rays, so to speak, of consciousness, and they would vary in quantity and quality as the opacity varied in degree.   Only at particular times and places would it seem that, as a matter of fact, the veil of nature can grow thin and rupturable enough for such effects to occur. But in those places gleams, however finite and unsatisfying, of the absolute life of the universe, are from time to time vouchsafed. Glows of feeling, glimpses of insight, and streams of knowledge and perception float into our finite world.

Admit now that *our brains* are such thin

and half-transparent places in the veil. What will happen? Why, as the white radiance comes through the dome, with all sorts of staining and distortion imprinted on it by the glass, or as the air now comes through my glottis determined and limited in its force and quality of its vibrations by the peculiarities of those vocal chords which form its gate of egress and shape it into my personal voice, even so the genuine matter of reality, the life of souls as it is in its fullness, will break through our several brains into this world in all sorts of restricted forms, and with all the imperfections and queernesses that characterize our finite individualities here below.

According to the state in which the brain finds itself, the barrier of its obstructiveness may also be supposed to rise or fall. It sinks so low, when the brain is in full activity, that a comparative flood of spiritual energy pours over. At other times, only such occasional waves of thought as heavy sleep permits get by. And when finally a brain stops acting altogether, or decays, that special stream of consciousness which it subserved will vanish entirely from this natural world. But the sphere of being that supplied the consciousness would still be intact ; and in that more real world with which, even whilst here, it was continuous, the consciousness might, in ways unknown to us, continue still.

You see that, on all these suppositions, our soul's life, as we here know it, would none the less in literal strictness be the function of the brain. The brain would be the independent variable, the mind would vary dependently on it. But such dependence on the brain for this natural life would in no wise make immortal life impossible, — it might be quite compatible with supernatural life behind the veil hereafter.

As I said, then, the fatal consequence is not coercive, the conclusion which materialism draws being due solely to its one-sided way of taking the word 'function.'

And, whether we care or not for immortality in itself, we ought, as mere critics doing police duty among the vagaries of mankind, to insist on the illogicality of a denial based on the flat ignoring of a palpable alternative. How much more ought we to insist, as lovers of truth, when the denial is that of such a vital hope of mankind!

In strict logic, then, the fangs of cerebralistic materialism are drawn. My words ought consequently already to exert a releasing function on your hopes. You *may* believe henceforward, whether you care to profit by the permission or not. But, as this is a very abstract argument, I think it will help its effect to say a word or two about the more concrete conditions of the case.

All abstract hypotheses sound unreal; and the abstract notion that our brains are colored lenses in the wall of nature, admitting light from the super-solar source, but at the same time tingeing and restricting it, has a thoroughly fantastic sound. What is it, you may ask, but a foolish metaphor? And how can such a function be imagined? Is n't the common materialistic notion vastly simpler? Is not consciousness really more comparable to a sort of steam, or perfume, or electricity, or nerve-glow, generated on the spot in its own peculiar vessel? Is it not more rigorously scientific to treat the brain's function as function of production?

The immediate reply is, that, if we are talking of science positively understood, function can mean nothing more than bare concomitant variation. When the brain-activities change in one way, consciousness changes in another; when the currents pour through the occipital lobes, consciousness *sees* things; when through the lower frontal region, consciousness *says* things to itself; when they stop, she goes to sleep, etc. In strict science, we can only write down the bare fact of concomitance; and all talk about either production or transmission, as the mode of

taking place, is pure superadded hypothesis, and metaphysical hypothesis at that,
for we can frame no more notion of the
details on the one alternative than on
the other. Ask for any indication of the
exact process either of transmission or
of production, and Science confesses her
imagination to be bankrupt. She has, so
far, not the least glimmer of a conjecture
or suggestion, — not even a bad verbal
metaphor or pun to offer. *Ignoramus*,
ignorabimus, is what most physiologists, in
the words of one of their number, will say
here. The production of such a thing as
consciousness in the brain, they will reply
with the late Berlin professor of physio-
logy, is the absolute world-enigma, — something so paradoxical and abnormal as to be
a stumbling block to Nature, and almost a
self-contradiction. Into the mode of production of steam in a tea-kettle we have
conjectural insight, for the terms that
change are physically homogeneous one
with another, and we can easily imagine

the case to consist of nothing but altera-
tions of molecular motion. But in the
production of consciousness by the brain,
the terms are heterogeneous natures altogether; and as far as our understanding
goes, it is as great a miracle as if we said,
Thought is 'spontaneously generated,' or
'created out of nothing.'

The theory of production is therefore
not a jot more simple or credible in itself
than any other conceivable theory. It is
only a little more popular. All that one
need do, therefore, if the ordinary materi-
alist should challenge one to explain how
the brain *can* be an organ for limiting and
determining to a certain form a consciousness elsewhere produced, is to retort with
a *tu quoque*, asking him in turn to explain how it can be an organ for producing
consciousness out of whole cloth. For
polemic purposes, the two theories are thus
exactly on a par.

But if we consider the theory of transmission in a wider way, we see that it has

certain positive superiorities, quite apart from its connection with the immortality question.

Just how the process of transmission may be carried on, is indeed unimaginable; but the outer relations, so to speak, of the process, encourage our belief. Consciousness in this process does not have to be generated *de novo* in a vast number of places. It exists already, behind the scenes, coeval with the world. The transmission-theory not only avoids in this way multiplying miracles, but it puts itself in touch with general idealistic philosophy better than the production-theory does. It should always be reckoned a good thing when science and philosophy thus meet.[5]

It puts itself also in touch with the conception of a 'threshold,' — a word with which, since Fechner wrote his book called 'Psychophysik,' the so-called 'new Psychology' has rung. Fechner imagines as the condition of consciousness a certain kind of psycho-physical movement, as he terms

it. Before consciousness can come, a certain degree of activity in the movement
must be reached. This requisite degree
is called the 'threshold;' but the height
of the threshold varies under different cir-
cumstances: it may rise or fall. When it
falls, as in states of great lucidity, we
grow conscious of things of which we
should be unconscious at other times;
when it rises, as in drowsiness, consciousness sinks in amount. This rising and
lowering of a psycho-physical threshold
exactly conforms to our notion of a per-
manent obstruction to the transmission
of consciousness, which obstruction may,
in our brains, grow alternately greater or
less.[6]

The transmission-theory also puts itself
in touch with a whole class of experiences that are with difficulty explained by
the production-theory. I refer to those ob-
scure and exceptional phenomena reported
at all times throughout human history,
which the 'psychical-researchers,' with

Mr. Frederic Myers at their head, are doing so much to rehabilitate;[7] such phenomena, namely, as religious conversions, providential leadings in answer to prayer, instantaneous healings, premonitions, apparitions at time of death, clairvoyant visions or impressions, and the whole range of mediumistic capacities, to say nothing of still more exceptional and incomprehensible things. If all our human thought be a function of the brain, then of course, if any of these things are facts, — and to my own mind some of them are facts, — we may not suppose that they can occur without preliminary brain-action. But the ordinary production-theory of consciousness is knit up with a peculiar notion of how brain-action *can* occur, — that notion being that all brain-action, without exception, is due to a prior action, immediate or remote, of the bodily sense-organs *on* the brain. Such action makes the brain produce sensations and mental images, and out of the sensations and images the higher forms of thought and

knowledge in their turn are framed. As
transmissionists, we also must admit this to
be the condition of all our usual thought.
Sense-action is what lowers the brain-bar-
rier. My voice and aspect, for instance,
strike upon your ears and eyes ; your brain
thereupon becomes more pervious, and
an awareness on your part of what I say
and who I am slips into this world from the
world behind the veil. But, in the mysterious phenomena to which I allude, it is
often hard to see where the sense-organs
can come in. A medium, for example, will
show knowledge of his sitter's private af-
fairs which it seems impossible he should
have acquired through sight or hearing, or
inference therefrom. Or you will have an
apparition of some one who is now dying
hundreds of miles away. On the production - theory one does not see from what
sensations such odd bits of knowledge are
produced. On the transmission - theory,
they don't have to be 'produced,' — they
exist ready - made in the transcendental

world, and all that is needed is an abnormal lowering of the brain-threshold to let them through. In cases of conversion, in providential leadings, sudden mental healings, etc., it seems to the subjects themselves of the experience as if a power from without, quite different from the ordinary action of the senses or of the sense-led mind, came into their life, as if the latter suddenly opened into that greater life in which it has its source. The word 'influx,' used in Swedenborgian circles, well describes this impression of new insight, or new willingness, sweeping over us like a tide. All such experiences, quite paradoxical and meaningless on the production-theory, fall very naturally into place on the other theory. We need only suppose the continuity of our consciousness with a mother sea, to allow for exceptional waves occasionally pouring over the dam. Of course the causes of these odd lowerings of the brain's threshold still remain a mystery on any terms.

Add, then, this advantage to the transmission-theory, — an advantage which I am
well aware that some of you will not rate
very high, — and also add the advantage of
not conflicting with a life hereafter, and I
hope you will agree with me that it has
many points of superiority to the more
familiar theory. It is a theory which, in
the history of opinion on such matters,
has never been wholly left out of account,
though never developed at any great length.
In the great orthodox philosophic tradition,
the body is treated as an essential condition
to the soul's life in this world of sense ; but
after death, it is said, the soul is set free,
and becomes a purely intellectual and non-
appetitive being. Kant expresses this idea
in terms that come singularly close to those
of our transmission-theory. The death of
the body, he says, may indeed be the end
of the sensational use of our mind, but only
the beginning of the intellectual use. " The
body," he continues, " would thus be, not
the cause of our thinking, but merely a

condition restrictive thereof, and, although essential to our sensuous and animal consciousness, it may be regarded as an impeder of our pure spiritual life.[8] And in a recent book of great suggestiveness and power, less well-known as yet than it deserves, — I mean 'Riddles of the Sphinx,' by Mr. F. C. S. Schiller of Oxford, late of Cornell University, — the transmissiontheory is defended at some length.[9]

But still, you will ask, in what positive way does this theory help us to realize our immortality in imagination? What we all wish to keep is just these individual restrictions, these selfsame tendencies and peculiarities that define us to ourselves and others, and constitute our identity, so called. Our finitenesses and limitations seem to be our personal essence; and when the finiting organ drops away, and our several spirits revert to their original source and resume their unrestricted condition, will they then be anything like those sweet streams of feeling which we know, and which even now our brains are sifting out from the great reservoir for our enjoyment here below? Such questions are truly living questions, and surely they must be seriously discussed by future lecturers upon this Ingersoll foundation. I hope, for my part, that more than one such lecturer will penetratingly discuss the conditions of our immortality, and tell us how much we may lose, and how much we may possibly gain, if its finiting outlines should be changed? If all determination is negation, as the philosophers say, it might well prove that the loss of some of the particular determinations which the brain imposes would not appear a matter for such absolute regret.

But into these higher and more transcendental matters I refuse to enter upon this occasion ; and I proceed, during the remainder of the hour, to treat of my second point. Fragmentary and negative it is, as my first one has been. Yet, between them, they do give to our belief in immortality a freer wing.

My second point is relative to the incredible and intolerable number of beings which, with our modern imagination, we must believe to be immortal, if immortality be true. I cannot but suspect that this, too, is a stumbling-block to many of my present audience. And it is a stumbling-block which I should thoroughly like to clear away.

It is, I fancy, a stumbling-block of altogether modern origin, due to the strain upon the quantitative imagination which recent scientific theories, and the moral feelings consequent upon them, have brought in their train.

For our ancestors the world was a small, and — compared with our modern sense of it — a comparatively snug affair. Six thousand years at most it had lasted. In its history a few particular human heroes, kings, ecclesiarchs, and saints stood forth very prominent, overshadowing the imagination with their claims and merits, so that not only they, but all who were associated familiarly with them, shone with a glamour which even the Almighty, it was supposed, must recognize and respect. These prominent personages and their associates were the nucleus of the immortal group; the minor heroes and saints of minor sects came next, and people without distinction formed a sort of background and filling in. The whole scene of eternity (so far, at least, as Heaven and not the nether place was concerned in it) never struck to the believer's fancy as an overwhelmingly large or inconveniently crowded stage. One might call this an aristocratic view of immortality; the immortals — I speak of Heaven exclusively, for an immortality of torment need not now concern us — were always an élite, a select and manageable number.

But, with our own generation, an entirely new quantitative imagination has swept over our western world. The theory of evolution now requires us to suppose a far vaster scale of times, spaces, and numbers

than our forefathers ever dreamed the cosmic process to involve. Human history
grows continuously out of animal history,
and goes back possibly even to the tertiary
epoch. From this there has emerged in-
sensibly a democratic view, instead of the
old aristocratic view, of immortality. For
our minds, though in one sense they may
have grown a little cynical, in another they
have been made sympathetic by the evolu-
tionary perspective. Bone of our bone and
flesh of our flesh are these half-brutish pre-
historic brothers. Girdled about with the
immense darkness of this mysterious universe even as we are, they were born and
died, suffered and struggled. Given over
to fearful crime and passion, plunged in the
blackest ignorance, preyed upon by hide-
ous and grotesque delusions, yet steadfastly
serving the profoundest of ideals in their
fixed faith that existence in any form is
better than non-existence, they ever res-
cued trimphantly from the jaws of ever-im-
minent destruction the torch of life, which,

thanks to them, now lights the world for us. How small indeed seem individual distinctions when we look back on these overwhelming numbers of human beings panting and straining under the pressure of that vital want! And how inessential in the eyes of God must be the small surplus of the individual's merit, swamped as it is in the vast ocean of the common merit of mankind, dumbly and undauntedly doing the fundamental duty and living the heroic life! We grow humble and reverent as we contemplate the prodigious spectacle. Not our differences and distinctions, — we feel — no, but our common animal essence of patience under suffering and enduring effort must be what redeems us in the Deity's sight. An immense compassion and kinship fill the heart. An immortality from which these inconceivable billions of fellow - strivers should be excluded becomes an irrational idea for us. That our superiority in personal refinement or in religious creed

should constitute a difference between ourselves and our messmates at life's banquet,
fit to entail such a consequential difference
of destiny as eternal life for us, and for
them torment hereafter, or death with the
beasts that perish, is a notion too absurd
to be considered serious. Nay, more, the
very beasts themselves — the wild ones
at any rate — are leading the heroic life
at all times. And a modern mind, ex-
panded as some minds are by cosmic emotion, by the great evolutionist vision of
universal continuity, hesitates to draw the
line even at man. If any creature lives
forever, why not all? — why not the patient brutes? So that a faith in immortality, if we are to indulge it, demands of us
nowadays a scale of representation so stu-
pendous that our imagination faints before
it, and our personal feelings refuse to rise
up and face the task. The supposition we
are swept along to is too vast, and, rather
than face the conclusion, we abandon the
premise from which it starts. We give up

our own immortality sooner than believe
that all the hosts of Hottentots and Aus-
tralians that have been, and shall ever be,
should share it with us *in secula seculorum.*
Life is a good thing on a reasonably copi-
ous scale ; but the very heavens themselves,
and the cosmic times and spaces, would
stand aghast, we think, at the notion of
preserving eternally such an ever-swelling
plethora and glut of it.

Having myself, as a recipient of modern
scientific culture, gone through a subjective experience like this, I feel sure that
it must also have been the experience of
many, perhaps of most, of you who listen
to my words.   But I have also come to see
that it harbors a tremendous fallacy ; and,
since the noting of the fallacy has set my
own mind free again, I have felt that one
service I might render to my listeners to-
night would be to point out where it lies.

It is the most obvious fallacy in the
world, and the only wonder is that all the
world should not see through it.   It is the

result of nothing but an invincible blindness from which we suffer, an insensibility to the inner significance of alien lives, and a conceit that would project our own incapacity into the vast cosmos, and measure the wants of the Absolute by our own puny needs. Our christian ancestors dealt with the problem more easily than we do. We, indeed, lack sympathy ; but they had a positive antipathy for these alien human creatures, and they naïvely supposed the Deity to have the antipathy, too. Being, as they were, 'heathen,' our forefathers felt a certain sort of joy in thinking that their Creator made them as so much mere fuel for the fires of hell. Our culture has humanized us beyond that point, but we cannot yet conceive them as our comrades in the fields of heaven. We have, as the phrase goes, *no use for them*, and it oppresses us to think of their survival. Take, for instance, all the Chinamen. Which of you here, my friends, sees any fitness in their eternal perpetuation unre-

duced in numbers? Surely not one of you.
At most, you might deem it well to keep a
few chosen specimens alive to represent an
interesting and peculiar variety of human-
ity ; but as for the rest, what comes in such
surpassing numbers, and what you can
only imagine in this abstract summary
collective manner, must be something of
which the units, you are sure, can have no
individual preciousness. God himself, you
think, can have no use for them. An immortality of every separate specimen must
be to him and to the universe as indiges-
tible a load to carry as it is to you. So,
engulfing the whole subject in a sort of
mental giddiness and nausea, you drift
along, first doubting that the mass can be
immortal, then losing all assurance in the
immortality of your own particular person,
precious as you all the while feel and realize the latter to be. This, I am sure, is
the attitude of mind of some of you before
me.

But is not such an attitude due to the

veriest lack and dearth of your imagination? You take these swarms of alien
kinsmen as they are *for you:* an external
picture painted on your retina, represent-
ing a crowd oppressive by its vastness and
confusion. As they are for you, so you
think they positively and absolutely are. *I*
feel no call for them, you say; therefore
there *is* no call for them. But all the
while, beyond this externality which is
your way of realizing them, they realize
themselves with the acutest internality,
with the most violent thrills of life. 'T is
you who are dead, stone-dead and blind
and senseless, in your way of looking on.
You open your eyes upon a scene of which
you miss the whole significance. Each of
these grotesque or even repulsive aliens is
animated by an inner joy of living as hot
or hotter than that which you feel beating
in your private breast. The sun rises and
beauty beams to light his path. To miss
the inner joy of him, as Stevenson says, is
to miss the whole of him.[10] Not a being

of the countless throng is there whose con-
tinued life is not called for, and called for
intensely, by the consciousness that ani-
mates the being's form. That *you* neither
realize nor understand nor call for it, that
you have no use for it, is an absolutely
irrelevant circumstance. That you have
a saturation-point of interest tells us nothing of the interests that absolutely are.
The Universe, with every living entity
which her resources create, creates at the
same time a call for that entity, and an
appetite for its continuance, — creates it,
if nowhere else, at least within the heart of
the entity itself. It is absurd to suppose,
simply because our private power of sympathetic vibration with other lives gives
out so soon, that in the heart of infinite
being itself there can be such a thing as
plethora, or glut, or supersaturation. It
is not as if there were a bounded room
where the minds in possession had to
move up or make place and crowd together
to accommodate new occupants. Each new

mind brings its own edition of the universe
of space along with it, its own room to in-
habit; and these spaces never crowd each
other, — the space of my imagination, for
example, in no way interferes with yours.
The amount of possible consciousness
seems to be governed by no law analogous
to that of the so-called conservation of energy in the material world. When one
man wakes up, or one is born, another does
not have to go to sleep, or die, in order to
keep the consciousness of the universe a
constant quantity. Professor Wundt, in
fact, in his 'System of Philosophy,' has
formulated a law of the universe which he
calls the law of increase of spiritual energy, and which he expressly opposes to
the law of conservation of energy in physical things.[11]   There seems no formal limit
to the positive increase of being in spiritual respects; and since spiritual being,
whenever it comes, affirms itself, expands
and craves continuance, we may justly and
literally say, regardless of the defects of

our own private sympathy, that the supply
of individual life in the universe can never
possibly, however immeasurable it may
become, exceed the demand.   The demand for that supply is there the moment
the supply itself comes into being, for the
beings supplied demand their own continuance.

I speak, you see, from the point of view
of all the other individual beings, realizing and enjoying inwardly their own existence.   If we are pantheists, we can
stop there.   We need, then, only say that
through them, as through so many diver-
sified channels of expression, the eternal
Spirit of the Universe affirms and realizes
its own infinite life.   But if we are theists,
we can go farther without altering the
result.   God, we can then say, has so in-
exhaustible a capacity for love that his call
and need is for a literally endless accu-
mulation of created lives.   He can never
faint or grow weary, as we should, under
the increasing supply.   His scale is infinite

in all things. His sympathy can never know satiety or glut.

I hope now that you agree with me that the tiresomeness of an over-peopled Heaven is a purely subjective and illusory notion, a sign of human incapacity, a remnant of the old narrow-hearted aristocratic creed. " Revere the Maker, lift thine eye up to his style and manners of the sky," and you will believe that this is indeed a democratic universe, in which your paltry exclusions play no regulative part. Was your taste consulted in the peopling of this globe ? How, then, should it be consulted as to the peopling of the vast City of God ? Let us put our hand over our mouth, like Job, and be thankful that in our personal littleness we ourselves are here at all. The Deity that suffers us, we may be sure, can suffer many another queer and wondrous and only half-delightful thing.

For my own part, then, so far as logic goes, I am willing that every leaf that ever grew in this world's forests and rustled in

the breeze should become immortal. It is
purely a question of fact : are the leaves
so, or not ? Abstract quantity, and the abstract needlessness in our eyes of so much
reduplication of things so much alike, have
no connection with the subject. For big-
ness and number and generic similarity
are only manners of our finite way of thinking ; and, considered in itself and apart
from our imagination, one scale of dimen-
sions and of numbers for the Universe is
no more miraculous or inconceivable than
another, the moment you grant to a universe the liberty to be at all, in place of the
Non-entity that might conceivably have
reigned.

The heart of being can have no exclusions akin to those which our poor little
hearts set up. The inner significance of
other lives exceeds all our powers of sympathy and insight. If we feel a significance in our own life which would lead us
spontaneously to claim its perpetuity, let
us be at least tolerant of like claims made

by other lives, however numerous, however unideal they may seem to us to be. Let us at any rate not decide adversely on our own claim, whose grounds we feel directly, because we cannot decide favorably on the alien claims, whose grounds we cannot feel at all. That would be letting blindness lay down the law to sight.

NOTES

NOTE I, page 9.

The gaps between the centres first recognized as motor and sensory — gaps which form in man two thirds of the surface of the hemispheres — are thus positively interpreted by Flechsig as intellectual centres strictly so called. [Compare his *Gehirn und Seele*, 2te Ausgabe, 1896, p. 23.] They have, he considers, a common type of microscopic structure; and the fibres connected with them are a month later in gaining their medullary sheath than are the fibres connected with the other centres. When disordered, they are the starting-point of the insanities, properly so called. Already Wernicke had defined insanity as disease of the organ of association, without so definitely pretending to circumscribe the latter — compare his *Grundriss der Psychiatrie*, 1894, p. 7. Flechsig goes so far as to say that he finds a difference of symptoms in general paralytics according as their frontal or their more posterior association-centres are diseased. Where it is the frontal centres, the patient's consciousness of self is more deranged than is his perception of purely objective relations. Where the posterior associative regions suffer, it is rather the patient's system of objective ideas that undergoes disintegration (*loc. cit.* pp. 89–91). In rodents Flechsig thinks there is a complete absence of association-centres, —the sensory centres touch each other. In carnivora and the lower monkeys the latter centres still exceed the association-centres in volume. Only in the katarhinal apes do we begin to find anything like the human type (p. 84).

In his little pamphlet, *Die Grenzen geistiger Gesundheit und Krankheit*, Leipzig, 1896, Flechsig ascribes the moral insensibility which is found in certain criminals to a diminution of internal pain-feeling due to degeneration of the 'Körperfühlsphäre,' that extensive anterior region first so named by Munk, in which he lays the seat of all the emotions and of the consciousness of self [*Gehirn und Seele*, pp. 62–68; *die Grenzen*, etc., pp. 31–39, 48]. — I give these references to Flechsig for concreteness' sake, not because his views are irreversibly made out.

NOTE 2, page 11.

So widespread is this conclusion in positivistic circles, so abundantly is it expressed in conversa-

tion, and so frequently implied in things that are
written, that I confess that my surprise was great
when I came to look into books for a passage
explicitly denying immortality on physiological
grounds, which I might quote to make my text
more concrete. I was unable to find anything
blunt and distinct enough to serve. I looked
through all the books that would naturally suggest
themselves, with no effect; and I vainly asked various psychological colleagues. And yet I should almost have been ready to take oath that I had read
several such passages of the most categoric sort
within the last decade. Very likely this is a false
impression, and it may be with this opinion as with
many others. The atmosphere is full of them;
many a writer's pages logically presuppose and
involve them; yet, if you wish to refer a student
to an express and radical statement that he may
employ as a text to comment on, you find almost
nothing that will do. In the present case there
are plenty of passages in which, in a general way,
mind is said to be conterminous with brain-function, but hardly one in which the author thereupon
explicitly denies the possibility of immortality.
The best one I have found is perhaps this: "Not
only consciousness, but every stirring of life, de-
pends on functions that go out like a flame when
nourishment is cut off. . . . The phenomena of

consciousness correspond, element for element, to the operations of special parts of the brain. . . . The destruction of any piece of the apparatus involves the loss of some one or other of the vital operations; and the consequence is that, as far as life extends, we have before us only an organic function, not a *Ding-an-sich*, or an expression of that imaginary entity the Soul. This fundamental proposition . . . carries with it the denial of the immortality of the soul, since, where no soul exists, its mortality or immortality cannot be raised as a question. . . . The function fills its time, — the flame illuminates and therein gives out its whole being. That is all; and verily that is enough. . . . Sensation has its definite organic conditions, and, as these decay with the natural decay of life, it is quite impossible for a mind accustomed to deal with realities to suppose any capacity of sensation as surviving when the machinery of our natural existence has stopped." [*E. Duhring: der Werth des Lebens*, 3d edition, pp. 48, 168.]

NOTE 3, page 12.

The philosophically instructed reader will notice that I have all along been placing myself at the ordinary dualistic point of view of natural science and of common sense. From this point of view mental facts like feelings are made of one kind of stuff or substance, physical facts of another. An absolute phenomenism, not believing such a dualism to be ultimate, may possibly end by solving some of the problems that are insoluble when propounded in dualistic terms. Meanwhile, since the physiological objection to immortality has arisen on the ordinary dualistic plane of thought, and since absolute phenomenism has as yet said nothing articulate enough to count about the matter, it is proper that my reply to the objection should be expressed in dualistic terms — leaving me free, of course, on any later occasion to make an attempt, if I wish, to transcend them and use different categories.

Now, on the dualistic assumption, one cannot see more than two really different sorts of dependence of our mind on our brain: Either

(1) The brain brings into being the very stuff of consciousness of which our mind consists; or else

(2) Consciousness preëxists as an entity, and the various brains give to it its various special forms.

If supposition 2 be the true one, and the stuff of mind preëxists, there are, again, only two ways of conceiving that our brain confers upon it the specifically human form. It may exist

(*a*) In disseminated particles; and then our brains are organs of concentration, organs for combining and massing these into resultant minds of personal form.   Or it may exist

(*b*) In vaster unities (absolute 'world-soul,' or something less); and then our brains are organs for separating it into parts and giving them finite form.

There are thus three possible theories of the brain's function, and no more.   We may name them, severally, —

1. The theory of production ;
2*a*. The theory of combination ;
2*b*. The theory of separation.

In the text of the lecture, theory number 2*b* (specified more particularly as the transmission-theory) is defended against theory number 1.   Theory 2*a*, otherwise known as the mind-dust or mind-stuff theory, is left entirely unnoticed for lack of time. I also leave it uncriticised in these notes, having already considered it, as fully as the so-far published forms of it may seem to call for, in my work, *The Principles of Psychology*, New York, Holt & Co., 1892, chapter VI.   I may say here, however, that Professor W. K. Clifford, one of the ablest champions of the combination-theory, and originator of the useful term 'mind-stuff,' considers that theory incompatible with individual immortality, and in his review of Stewart's and Tait's book, *The Unseen Universe*, thus expresses his conviction : —

" The laws connecting consciousness with changes in the brain are very definite and precise, and their necessary consequences are not to be evaded. . . . Consciousness is a complex thing made up of elements, a stream of feelings. The action of the brain is also a complex thing made up of elements, a stream of nerve-messages. For every feeling in consciousness there is at the same time a nerve-message in the brain. . . . Consciousness is not a simple thing, but a complex ; it is the combination of feelings into a stream. It exists at the same time with the combination of nerve-messages into a stream. If individual feeling always goes with individual nerve-message, if combination or stream of feelings always goes with stream of nerve-messages, does it not follow that, when the stream of nerve-messages is broken up, the stream of feelings will be broken up also, will no longer form a consciousness ? Does it not follow that, when the messages themselves are broken up, the individual feelings will be resolved into still simpler elements ? The force of this evidence is not to be weakened by any number of spiritual bodies. Inexorable facts connect our consciousness with this body that we know ; and that not merely as a whole, but the parts of it are connected severally with parts of our brain-action. If there is any similar connection with a spiritual body, it only follows that the spiritual body must die at the same time with the natural one." [*Lectures and Essays*, vol. i. p. 247-49. Compare also passages of similar purport in vol. ii. pp. 65-70.]

NOTE 4, page 13.

The theory of production, or materialistic theory, seldom ventures to formulate itself very distinctly. Perhaps the following passage from Cabanis is as explicit as anything one can find : —

" To acquire a just idea of the operations from which thought results, we must consider the brain as a particular organ specially destined to produce it; just as the stomach and intestines are destined to operate digestion, the liver to filter bile, the parotid and maxillary glands to prepare the salivary juices. The impressions, arriving in the brain, force it to enter into activity; just as the alimentary materials, falling into the stomach, excite it to a more abundant secretion of gastric juice, and to the movements which result in their own solution. The function proper to the first organ is that of receiving [*percevoir*] each particular impression, of attaching signs to it, of combining the different impressions, of comparing them with each other, of drawing from them judgments and resolves; just as the function of the other organ is to act upon the nutritive substances whose presence excites it, to dissolve them, and to assimilate their juices to our nature.

" Do you say that the organic movements by which the brain exercises these functions are unknown ? I reply that the action by which the nerves of the stomach determine the different operations which constitute digestion, and the manner in which they confer so active a solvent power upon the gastric juice, are equally hidden from our scrutiny. We see the food-materials fall into this viscus with their own proper qualities ; we see them emerge with new qualities, and we infer that the stomach is really the author of this alteration. Similarly we see the impressions reaching the brain by the intermediation of the nerves ; they then are isolated and without coherence. The viscus enters into action ; it acts upon them, and soon it emits [*renvoie*] them metamorphosed into ideas, to which the language of physiognomy or gesture, or the signs of speech and writing, give an outward expression. We conclude, then, with an equal certitude, that the brain digests, as it were, the impressions ; that it performs organically the secretion of thought." [*Rapports du Physique et du Moral*, 8th edition, 1844, p. 137.]

It is to the ambiguity of the word ' impression ' that such an account owes whatever plausibility it may seem to have. More recent forms of the production-theory have shown a tendency to liken thought to a 'force' which the brain exerts, or to a 'state' into which it passes. Herbert Spencer, for instance, writes : —

"The law of metamorphosis, which holds among the physical forces, holds equally between them and the mental forces. . . . How this metamorphosis takes place; how a force existing as motion, heat, or light can become a mode of consciousness ; how it is possible for aerial vibrations to generate the sensation we call sound, or for the forces liberated by chemical changes in the brain to give rise to emotion, — these are mysteries which it is impossible to fathom. But they are not profounder mysteries than the transformations of the physical forces into each other." [*First Principles, 2nd Edition*, p. 217.]

So Büchner says: " Thinking must be regarded as a special mode of general natural motion, which is as characteristic of the substance of the central nervous elements as the motion of contraction is of the nerve-substance, or the motion of light is of the universal-ether. . . . That thinking is and must be a mode of motion is not merely a postulate of logic, but a proposition which has of late been demonstrated experimentally. . . . Various ingenious experiments have proved that the swiftest thought that we are able to evolve occupies at least the eighth or tenth part of a second." [*Force and Matter*, New York, 1891, p. 241.]

Heat and light, being modes of motion, 'phosphorescence' and 'incandescence' are phenomena to which consciousness has been likened by the production-theory: "As one sees a metallic rod, placed in a glowing furnace, gradually heat itself, and — as the undulations of the caloric grow more and more frequent — pass successively from the shades of bright red to dark red (*sic*), to white, and develope, as its temperature rises, heat and light, — so the living sensitive cells, in presence of the incitations that solicit them, exalt themselves progressively as to their most interior sensibility, enter into a phase of erethism, and at a certain number of vibrations, set free (*dégagent*) pain as a physiological expression of this same sensibility superheated to a red-white." [J. Luys: *le Cerveau*, p. 91.]

In a similar vein Mr. Percival Lowell writes: "When we have, as we say, an idea, what happens inside of us is probably something like this: the neural current of molecular change passes up the nerves, and through the ganglia reaches at last the cortical cells. . . . When it reaches the cortical cells, it finds a set of molecules which are not so accustomed to this special change. The current encounters resistance, and in overcoming this resistance it causes the cells to glow. This white-heating of the cells we call consciousness. Consciousness, in short, is probably nerve-glow." [*Occult Japan*, Boston, 1895, p. 311.]

NOTE 5, page 23.

The transmission-theory connects itself very naturally with that whole tendency of thought known as transcendentalism. Emerson, for example, writes: "We lie in the lap of immense intelligence, which makes us receivers of its truth ana organs of its activity. When we discern justice, when we discern truth, we do nothing of ourselves, but allow a passage to its beams." [*Self-Reliance*, p. 56.] But it is not necessary to identify the consciousness postulated in the lecture, as preëxisting behind the scenes, with the Absolute Mind of transcendental Idealism, although, indeed, the notion of it might lead in that direction. The absolute Mind of transcendental Idealism is one integral Unit, one single World-mind. For the purposes of my lecture, however, there might be many minds behind the scenes as well as one. All that the transmission-theory absolutely requires is that they should transcend *our* minds, — which thus come from *something* mental that pre-exists, and is larger than themselves.

Note 6, page 24.

Fechner's conception of a 'psycho-physical threshold' as connected with his 'wave-scheme' is little known to English readers. I accordingly subjoin it, in his own words, abridged : —

"The psychically one is connected with a physically many ; the physically many contract psychically into a one, a simple, or at least a more simple. Otherwise expressed : the psychically unified and simple are resultants of physical multiplicity ; the physically manifold gives unified or simple results. . . .

"The facts which are grouped together under these expressions, and which give them their meaning, are as follows : . . . With our two hemispheres we think singly ; with the identical parts of our two retinæ we see singly. . . . The simplest sensation of light or sound in us is connected with processes which, since they are started and kept up by outer oscillations, must themselves be somehow of an oscillatory nature, although we are wholly unaware of the separate phases and oscillations. . . .

"It is certain, then, that some unified or simple psychic resultants depend on physical multiplicity. But, on the other hand, it is equally certain that the multiplicities of the physical world do not always combine into a simple psychical resultant,

— no, not even when they are compounded in a single bodily system. Whether they may not nevertheless combine into a *unified* resultant is a matter for opinion, since one is always free to ask whether the entire world, as such, may not have some unified psychic resultant. But of any such resultant we at least have no consciousness. . . .

"For brevity's sake, let us distinguish *psychophysical continuity* and *discontinuity* from each other. Continuity, let us say, takes place so far as a physical manifold gives a unified or simple psychic resultant; discontinuity, so far as it gives a distinguishable multiplicity of such resultants. Inasmuch, however, as, within the unity of a more general consciousness or phenomenon of consciousness, there still may be a multiplicity distinguished, the continuity of a more general consciousness does not exclude the discontinuity of particular phenomena.

"One of the most important problems and tasks of Psycho-physics now is this: to determine the conditions (*Gesichtspunkte*) under which the cases of continuity and of discontinuity occur.

"Whence comes it that different organisms have separate consciousnesses, although their bodies are just as much connected by general Nature as the parts of a single organism are with each other, and these latter give a single conscious resultant? Of course we can say that the connection is more intimate between the parts of an organism than between the organisms of Nature. But what do we mean by a more intimate connection? Can an absolute difference of result depend on anything so relative? And does not Nature as a whole show as strict a connection as any organism does, — yea, one even more indissoluble? And the same questions come up within each organism. How comes it that, with different nerve-fibres of touch and sight, we distinguish different space-points, but with one fibre distinguish nothing, although the different fibres are connected in the brain just as much as the parts are in the single fibre? We may again call the latter connection the more *intimate*, but then the same sort of question will arise again.

"Unquestionably the problem which here lies before Psycho - physics cannot be *sharply* answered; but we may establish a general point of view for its treatment, consistently with what we laid down in a former chapter on the relations of more general with more particular phenomena of consciousness."

[The earlier passage is here inserted:] "The essential principle is this: That human psycho-physical activity must exceed a certain intensity for any waking consciousness at all to occur, and

that during the waking state any particular specification of the said activity (whether spontaneous or
due to stimulation), which is capable of occasion-
ing a particular specification of consciousness, must
exceed in its turn a certain further degree of intensity for the consciousness actually to arise. . . .

" This state of things (in itself a mere fact need-
ing no picture) may be made clearer by an image
or scheme, and also more concisely spoken of.
Imagine the whole psycho-physical activity of man
to be a wave, and the degree of this activity to be
symbolized by the height of the wave above a hori-
zontal basal line or surface, to which every psycho-
physically active point contributes an ordinate. . . .
The whole form and evolution of the consciousness will then depend on the rising and falling of
this wave; the intensity of the consciousness at
any time on the wave's height at that time; and
the height must always *somewhere* exceed a certain
limit, which we will call a *threshold*, if waking consciousness is to exist at all.

" Let us call this wave the *total wave*, and the
threshold in question the *principal threshold*."

[Since our various states of consciousness recur,
some in long, some in short periods], "we may
represent such a long period as that of the slowly
fluctuating condition of our general wakefulness and
the general direction of our attention as a wave

that slowly changes the place of its summit. If we call this the *under-wave*, then the movements of shorter period, on which the more special conscious states depend, can be symbolized by wavelets superposed upon the under-wave, and we can call these *over-waves*. They will cause all sorts of modifications of the under-wave's surface, and the total wave will be the resultant of both sets of waves.

"The greater, now, the strength of the movements of short period, the amplitude of the oscillations of the psycho-physical activity, the higher will the crests of the wavelets that represent them rise above, and the lower will their valleys sink below the surface of the under-wave that bears them. And these heights and depressions must exceed a certain limit of quantity which we may call the *upper threshold*, before the special mental state which is correlated with them can appear in consciousness " [pp. 454–456].

" So far now as we symbolize any system of psycho-physical activity, to which a generally unified or principal consciousness corresponds, by the image of a total wave rising with its crest above a certain 'threshold,' we have a means of schematizing in a single diagram the physical solidarity of all these psycho-physical systems throughout Nature, together with their pyscho - physical discontinuity.

For we need only draw all the waves so that they run into each other below the threshold, whilst above it they appear distinct, as in the figure below.

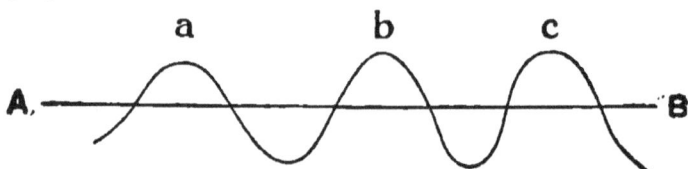

"In this figure *a*, *b*, *c* stand for three organisms, or rather for the total waves of psycho-physical activity of three organisms, whilst A B represents the threshold. In each wave the part that rises above the threshold is an integrated thing, and is connected with a single consciousness. Whatever lies below the threshold, being unconscious, separates the conscious crests, although it is still the means of physical connection.

"In general terms: wherever a psycho-physical total wave is continuous with itself above the threshold, there we find the unity or identity of a consciousness, inasmuch as the connection of the psychical phenomena which correspond to the parts of the wave also appears in consciousness. Whenever, on the contrary, total waves are disconnected, or connected only underneath the threshold, the corresponding consciousness is broken, and no connection between its several parts appears. More briefly: consciousness is continuous or discontinuous, unified or discrete, according as the psycho-physical total waves that subserve it are themselves continuous or discontinuous above the threshold. . . .

"If, in the diagram, we should raise the entire line of waves so that not only the crests but the valleys appeared above the threshold, then these latter would appear only as depressions in one great continuous wave above the threshold, and the discontinuity of the consciousness would be converted into continuity. We of course cannot bring this about. We might also squeeze the wave together so that the valleys should be pressed up, and the crests above the threshold flow into a line; then the discretely-feeling organisms would have become a singly - feeling organism. This, again, Man cannot voluntarily bring about, but it is brought about in Man's nature. His two halves, the right one and the left one, are thus united; and the number of segments of radiates and articulates show that more than two parts can be thus psycho-physically conjoined. One need only cut them asunder, *i. e.* interpolate another part of nature between them under the threshold, and they break into two separately conscious beings." . . . [*Elemente der Psychophysik*, 1860, vol. ii. pp. 526–530.]

One sees easily how, on Fechner's wave-scheme,

a world-soul may be expressed. All psycho-physical activity being continuous 'below the threshold,' the consciousness might also become continuous if the threshold sank low enough to uncover all the waves. The threshold throughout nature in general is, however, very high, so the consciousness that gets over it is of the discontinuous form.

Note 7, page 25.

See the long series of articles by Mr. Myers in the *Proceedings of the Society for Psychical Research*, beginning in the third volume with automatic writing, and ending in the latest volumes with the higher manifestations of knowledge by mediums. Mr. Myers's theory of the whole range of phenomena is, that our normal consciousness is in continuous connection with a greater consciousness of which we do not know the extent, and to which he gives, in its relation to the particular person, the not very felicitous name — though no better one has been proposed — of his or her 'subliminal' self.

Note 8, page 29.

See *Kritik der reinen Vernunft*, second edition, p. 809.

Note 9, page 29.

I subjoin a few extracts from Mr. Schiller's work: " Matter is an admirably calculated machinery for regulating, limiting, and restraining the consciousness which it encases. . . . If the material encasement be coarse and simple, as in the lower organisms, it permits only a little intelligence to permeate through it; if it is delicate and complex, it leaves more pores and exits, as it were, for the manifestations of consciousness. . . . On this analogy, then, we may say that the lower animals are still entranced in the lower stage of brute *lethargy*, while we have passed into the higher phase of *somnambulism*, which already permits us strange glimpses of a lucidity that divines the realities of a transcendent world. And this gives the final answer to Materialism: it consists in showing in detail . . . that Materialism is a hysteron proteron, a putting of the cart before the horse, which may be rectified by just inverting the connection between Matter and Consciousness. Matter is not that which *produces* Consciousness, but that which *limits* it, and confines its intensity within certain limits: material organization does not construct consciousness out of arrangements of atoms, but contracts its manifestation within the sphere which it permits. This explanation . . . admits the connection of Matter and Consciousness, but contends that the course of interpretation must proceed in the contrary direction. Thus it will fit the facts alleged in favor of Materialism equally well, besides enabling us to understand facts which Materialism rejected as 'supernatural.' It explains the lower by the higher, Matter by Spirit, instead of *vice versa*, and thereby attains to an explanation which is ultimately tenable, instead of one which is ultimately absurd. And it is an explanation the possibility of which no evidence in favor of Materialism can possibly affect. For if, *e. g.*, a man loses consciousness as soon as his brain is injured, it is clearly as good an explanation to say the injury to the brain destroyed the mechanism by which the manifestation of the consciousness was rendered possible, as to say that it destroyed the seat of consciousness. On the other hand, there are facts which the former theory suits far better. If, *e. g.*, as sometimes happens, the man, after a time, more or less, recovers the faculties of which the injury to his brain had deprived him, and that not in consequence of a renewal of the injured part, but in consequence of the inhibited functions being performed by the vicarious action of other parts, the easiest explanation certainly is that, after a time, consciousness constitutes the remaining parts into a mechanism capable of acting as a substitute for the lost parts. And again, if the body is a mechanism for inhibiting consciousness, for preventing the full powers of the Ego from being prematurely actualized, it will be necessary to invert also our ordinary ideas on the subject of memory, and to account for forgetfulness instead of for memory. It will be during life that we drink the bitter cup of Lethe, it will be with our brain that we are enabled to forget. And this will serve to explain not only the extraordinary memories of the drowning and the dying generally, but also the curious hints which experimental psychology occasionally affords us that nothing is ever forgotten wholly and beyond recall." [*Riddles of the Sphinx*, London, Swan Sonnenschein, 1891, p. 293 ff.]

Mr. Schiller's conception is much more complex in its relations than the simple 'theory of transmission' postulated in my lecture, and to do justice to it the reader should consult the original work.

NOTE 10, page 39.

I beg the reader to peruse R. L. Stevenson's magnificent little essay entitled 'The Lantern Bearers,' reprinted in the collection entitled *Across the Plains*. The truth is that we are doomed, by the fact that we are practical beings with very limited tasks to attend to, and special ideals to look after, to be absolutely blind and insensible to the inner feelings, and to the whole inner significance of lives that are different from our own. Our opinion of the worth of such lives is absolutely wide of the mark, and unfit to be counted at all.

NOTE II, page 41.

W. Wundt: *System der Philosophie*, Leipzig, Engelmann, 1889, p. 315.

THE END.

The Riverside Press

CAMBRIDGE, MASSACHUSETTS U. S. A.
ELECTROTYPED AND PRINTED BY
H. O. HOUGHTON AND CO.

www.ingramcontent.com/pod-product-compliance
Lightning Source LLC
Chambersburg PA
CBHW021427090426
42742CB00009B/1286